Editor
Eric Migliaccio

Editor in Chief
Karen J. Goldfluss, M.S. Ed.

Creative Director
Sarah M. Smith

Cover Artist
Barb Lorseyedi

Art Coordinator
Renée Mc Elwee

Illustrator
Clint McKnight

Imaging
James Edward Grace

Publisher
Mary D. Smith, M.S. Ed.

Author

Heather Wolpert-Gawron

For correlations to Common Core State Standards, see page 8 of this book or visit *http://www.teachercreated.com/standards/*.

Teacher Created Resources
6421 Industry Way
Westminster, CA 92683
www.teachercreated.com
ISBN: 978-1-4206-3826-4
© 2014 Teacher Created Resources
Made in U.S.A.

Table of Contents

Introduction

Reading and comprehending nonfiction or informational text is a challenge. Not everyone can do it well, and it needs to be specifically taught. Students who are great at reading narratives like *Lord of the Rings* or *The Princess Diaries* may still quiver at the possibility of having to understand instructions on uploading an assignment to DropBox. Students who love reading historical fiction may be fearful of reading history. Students who, with flashlight in hand, hide beneath their sheets reading the end of a science-fiction book may glaze over at the sight of an actual factual science article.

Nevertheless, informational text is all around us, and reading it well just takes working out a certain muscle — an informational-text muscle, if you will.

This book is meant to be an informational-muscle gym. Each activity is meant to build in complexity, and each activity is meant to push students in both their reading and their ability to display what they understand about what they read.

In addition to a practice passage, there are 18 reading selections contained in this book. The selections are separated into units, based on their subject matter. As a result, no matter the content area you teach, you will find applicable selections here on which your students can practice.

It doesn't matter what state you teach in, what grade level you teach, or what subject you teach; this book will aid students in understanding more deeply the difficult task of reading informational and nonfiction texts.

Reading Comprehension and the Common Core

The Common Core Standards are here, and with them come a different way to think about reading comprehension. In the past, reading informational text had been compartmentalized, each piece an isolated activity. The Common Core way of thinking is slightly different.

The goal is for students to read different genres and selections of text, pull them together in their heads, and be able to derive a theme or topic that may be shared by them all. In other words, a student may be given three different texts from three different points of view or three different genre standpoints and then have to think about their own thoughts on the subject.

Perhaps a student looks at the following:

1. Instructions on downloading an image from a digital camera
2. A biography about a famous photographer
3. A Google search history on the invention of the camera from the past to the present

Then, from those pieces, the student must pull a common theme or opinion on the topic.

Introduction (cont.)

Reading Comprehension and the Common Core (cont.)

But to be able to synthesize text (put the thoughts together), a student must first be able to read individual texts and analyze them (pull them apart). That's where this series of books comes in.

Nonfiction Reading Comprehension for the Common Core helps students to hone in on a specific piece of text, identify what's the most important concept in that piece, and answer questions about that specific selection. This will train your students for the bigger challenge that will come later in their schooling: viewing multiple texts and shaking out the meaning of them all.

If you are a public-school teacher, you may be in a state that has adopted the Common Core Standards. Use the selections in this book as individual reading-comprehension activities or pair them with similarly themed selections from other genres to give students a sense of how they will have to pull understanding from the informational, text-heavy world around us.

Copy the individual worksheets as is; or, if you are looking for a more Common Core-aligned format, mimic the Common Core multiple-choice assessments that are coming our way by entering the questions into websites that can help create computer adaptive tests (CATs).

CATs are assessments that allow a student to answer a question, which, depending on whether they answered it correctly or not, leads them to the next question that may be more geared to his or her level. In other words, each student will be taking a differentiated assessment that will end up indicating if a student is capable of answering "Novice" questions up to "Expert" questions.

There are many websites out there that can help you develop assessments to mimic those planned. Create the quiz and embed it into your class webpage or document:

Here are just a couple:

- *http://www.gotoquiz.com/create.html*
- *http://www.quibblo.com/*

Use the selections from this book, and then enter the corresponding questions into the quiz generators. We have identified questions that are higher or lower in level by assigning them a "weight" (from single-weight up through triple-weight). This weight system provides a glimpse of how hard a student should work in order to answer the question correctly. (For more information, read "Leveled Questions" on page 5.)

Regardless of how you choose to use this book, introducing students to the informational world at large is an important way to help them build skills that they will use throughout their schooling and beyond.

Introduction *(cont.)*

Leveled Questions

As you go through this book, you will notice that each question that students will be answering is labeled with icons that look like weights. These icons represent different levels of difficulty. The levels are based on Costa's Levels of Questioning.

The questions in this book are divided into three levels:

Level 1	**Level 2**	**Level 3**
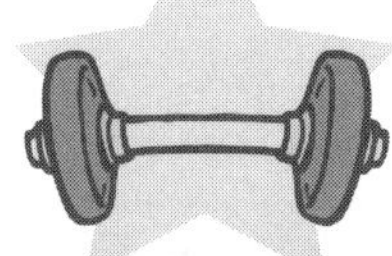	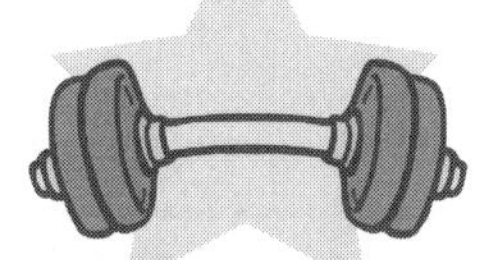	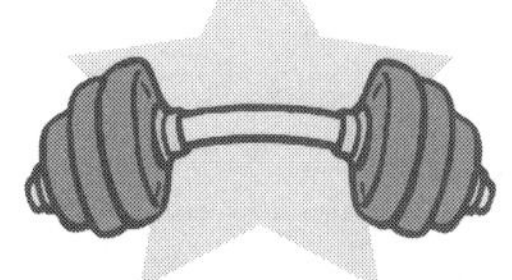
These include sentence stems that ask students to . . .	*These include sentence stems that ask students to . . .*	*These include sentence stems that ask students to . . .*
Recite **Define** **Describe** **List**	**Infer** **Compare/Contrast** **Sequence** **Categorize**	**Judge** **Evaluate** **Create** **Hypothesize** **Predict**

The icons are a visual way to make these levels clear to students. That is important because students need to be able to recognize that some questions may require more effort and thought to answer.

Now, most of the multiple-choice questions in this book happen to fall into the Level 1 and Level 2 categories. That is pretty standard for multiple-choice questions. After all, how can asking to create something be defined by an A, B, C, or D answer? However, we may have found a way around that.

At the end of each worksheet is a place for students to develop their own questions about the material they have just read. This brings in a deeper-thinking opportunity. Having your students ask higher-level questions is a great way for assessing their comprehension of what they have read. The deeper the student's question, the deeper his or her understanding of the material.

A student handout called "The Questioning Rubric" is provided on page 6. It serves two purposes:

- It gives your students concrete examples of the elements that make up the different levels of questions.
- It gives you, the teacher, a way to determine whether a student-generated question is a low- or high-level inquiry.

The goal of a student is to ask more challenging questions of oneself. The goal of the teacher is to be able to track better the level of production for each student. This book helps do both.

Introduction _(cont.)_

The Questioning Rubric

Answering questions is one way of proving you understand a reading selection. However, creating your very own questions about the selection might be an even better way. Developing thoughtful, high-level questions can really display your understanding of what you have read, and it also makes other students think about the reading passage in a unique way.

So what types of questions can you ask? There are three levels of questions, and for each one there is a different amount of work your brain must do to answer the question. We've chosen to use a symbol of a weight in order to represent this amount. Consult this chart when thinking about what defines a great question as compared to a so-so one.

Icon	Description
	A single weight represents a **Level 1** question that doesn't require much brainpower to answer correctly. The question only asks readers to tell what they know about the selection. For example, any inquiry that asks for a simple "Yes or No" or "True or False" response is a Level 1 question.
	A double weight represents a **Level 2** question that requires you to use a little more brain sweat. (Ewww!) This question asks readers to think a little beyond the passage. It may require some analysis, inference, or interpretation. Questions involving comparing/contrasting or sequencing often fall here.
	A **Level 3** question really makes you work for its answer. These questions allow you to show off your knowledge of a topic by asking you to create, wonder, judge, evaluate, and/or apply what you know to what you think. These types of questions are much more open-ended than Level 1 or Level 2 questions.

Don't be scared to sweat a little in answering or developing Level 3 questions. Working out your brain in this way will help prepare you for some heavy lifting later on in life. So as you progress through this book, use this rubric as a resource to make sure your questions are as high-level as possible.

Need help getting started? The following sentence stems will give you ideas about how to create questions for each level.

Level 1
- Write the definition of…
- Describe how ______ is…
- List the details that go into…

Level 2
- What can you infer from ______?
- Compare ______ with ______.
- Contrast ______ with ______.
- Write the steps in sequence from ______.
- Place ______ in the right category.

Level 3
- How would you judge the ______?
- How would you evaluate the ______?
- How can you create a ______?
- Hypothesize what would happen if ______.
- What do you predict will happen in ______?

Introduction *(cont.)*

Achievement Graph

As you correct your responses in this book, track how well you improve. Calculate how many answers you got right after each worksheet and mark your progress here based on the number of weights each question was worth. For instance, if you get the first problem correct and it is worth two weights, then write "2" in the first column. Do this for each column and add up your total at the end.

Reading Passage	1	2	3	4	Total
"The Birth of Silly Putty"					
"What is Extinction?"					
"Gentle Giant of the Sea"					
"The History of Balloon Flight"					
"What Is a Geode?"					
"The First Observatory"					
"A Storytelling Tradition"					
"The Guiding Rose"					
"Women in the Civil War"					
"Which Holiday Is This?"					
"A Writer Who Lives On"					
"Ben's Words of Wisdom"					
"An Early Start on Success"					
"The Writer on Every Shelf"					
"Racing Into History"					
"A Better Way to Search"					
"Reading an Infographic"					
"A Way to Show Time"					
"A Show of Shadows"					

Common Core State Standards

The lessons and activities included in *Nonfiction Reading Comprehension for the Common Core, Grade 5* meet the following Common Core State Standards. (©Copyright 2010. National Governors Association Center for Best Practices and Council of Chief State School Officers. All rights reserved.) For more information about the Common Core State Standards, go to *http://www.corestandards.org/* or visit *http://www.teachercreated.com/standards/*.

Informational Text Standards	
Key Ideas and Details	**Pages**
CCSS.ELA.RI.5.3. Explain the relationships or interactions between two or more individuals, events, ideas, or concepts in a historical, scientific, or technical text based on specific information in the text.	10–47
Craft and Structure	**Pages**
CCSS.ELA.RI.5.4. Determine the meaning of general academic and domain-specific words and phrases in a text relevant to a grade 5 topic or subject area	10–47
Range of Reading and Level of Text Complexity	**Pages**
CCSS.ELA.RI.5.10. By the end of the year, read and comprehend informational texts, including history/social studies, science, and technical texts, at the high end of the grades 4–5 text complexity band independently and proficiently.	10–47
Foundational Skills	
Phonics and Word Recognition	**Pages**
CCSS.ELA.RF.5.3. Know and apply grade-level phonics and word-analysis skills in decoding words.	10–47
Fluency	**Pages**
CCSS.ELA.RF.5.4. Read with sufficient accuracy and fluency to support comprehension.	10–47
Language Standards	
Conventions of Standard English	**Pages**
CCSS.ELA.L.5.1. Demonstrate command of the conventions of standard English grammar and usage when writing or speaking.	11–47
CCSS.ELA.L.5.2. Demonstrate command of the conventions of standard English capitalization, punctuation, and spelling when writing.	11–47
Knowledge of Language	**Pages**
CCSS.ELA.L.5.3. Use knowledge of language and its conventions when writing, speaking, reading, or listening.	10–47
Vocabulary Acquisition and Use	**Pages**
CCSS.ELA.L.5.4. Determine or clarify the meaning of unknown and multiple-meaning words and phrases based on *grade 5 reading and content*, choosing flexibly from a range of strategies.	10–47
CCSS.ELA.L.5.5. Demonstrate understanding of figurative language, word relationships, and nuances in word meanings.	10–47

Multiple-Choice Test-Taking Tips

Some multiple-choice questions are straightforward and easy. "I know the answer!" your brain yells right away. Some questions, however, stump even the most prepared student. In cases like that, you have to make an educated guess. An educated guess is a guess that uses what you know to help guide your attempt. You don't put your hand over your eyes and pick a random letter! You select it because you've thought about the format of the question, the word choice, the other possible answers, and the language of what's being asked. By making an educated guess, you're increasing your chances of guessing correctly. Whenever you are taking a multiple-choice assessment, you should remember to follow the rules below:

1. Read the directions. It's crucial. You may assume you know what is being asked, but sometimes directions can be tricky when you least expect them to be.

2. Read the questions before you read the passage. Doing this allows you to read the text through a more educated and focused lens. For example, if you know that you will be asked to identify the main idea, you can be on the lookout for that ahead of time.

3. Don't skip a question. Instead, try to make an educated guess. That starts with crossing off the ones you definitely know are not the correct answer. For instance, if you have four possible answers (A, B, C, D) and you can cross off two of them immediately, you've doubled your chances of guessing correctly. If you don't cross off any obvious ones, you would only have a 25% chance of guessing right. However, if you cross off two, you now have a 50% chance!

4. Read carefully for words like *always*, *never*, *not*, *except*, and *every*. Words like these are there to make you stumble. They make the question very specific. Sometimes an answer can be right some of the time, but if a word like *always* or *every* is in the question, the answer must be right *all of the time*.

5. After reading a question, try to come up with the answer first in your head before looking at the possible answers. That way, you will be less likely to bubble or click something you aren't sure about.

6. In questions with an "All of the Above" answer, think of it this way: if you can identify at least two that are correct, then "All of the Above" is probably the correct answer.

7. In questions with a "None of the Above" answer, think of it this way: if you can identify at least two that are *not* correct, then "None of the Above" is probably the correct answer.

8. Don't keep changing your answer. Unless you are sure you made a mistake, usually the first answer you chose is the right one.

The Birth of Silly Putty

Stretch it. Bounce it. Smoosh it. Silly Putty is one of history's most fun toys, but it did not start that way. It was invented by accident in 1943. During World War II, the United States was short on rubber. A substitute was needed. A man named James Wright tried mixing boric acid with silicone oil. A bouncy new substance was born, and Wright named it "Nutty Putty."

It wasn't until 1950 that this new stuff became well known. That is when a man named Peter Hodgson bought the rights to make it. He renamed it "Silly Putty" and sold it around the U.S. People loved it! It became a hit with both children and adults.

What can you do with Silly Putty? It can be rolled into a ball. It can be used to pick up pet hair from fabrics. It can be flattened out and pressed to a book. When this is done, the words from the book will appear on the putty's pink surface. Do you have a wobbly table? A little wad under the leg will fix that. Astronauts have even used Silly Putty to repair things in space!

As you can see, Silly Putty has come a long way. About 600 lbs. of it is now produced every day. It is even on display in the Smithsonian Institute. You can find it in the same exhibit hall as the washing machine, Kevlar, and the jukebox. Perhaps "Silly Putty" isn't so silly after all!

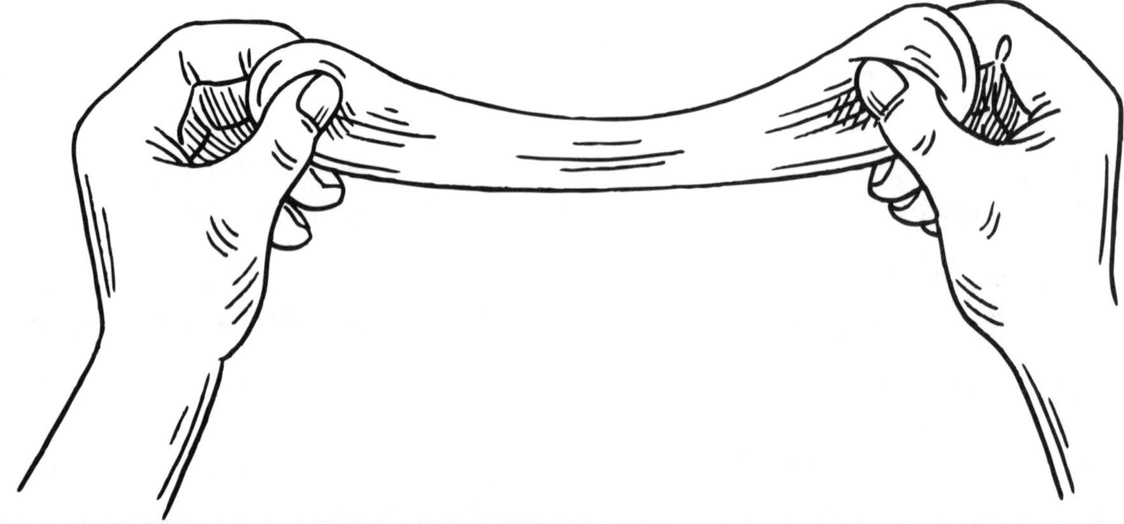

Answer the following questions about the story "The Birth of Silly Putty." The weights show you how hard you will need to work to find each answer.

1. What was James Wright working on when he discovered Silly Putty?

    Ⓐ a new tank for soldiers in World War II

    Ⓑ a new toy for children to play with

    Ⓒ a new way for people to secure their wobbly furniture

    Ⓓ a new substitute for rubber

2. What were the two chemicals that became Silly Putty?

    Ⓐ boric acid and ammonia   Ⓒ boric acid and silicone oil

    Ⓑ silicone oil and hydrogen peroxide   Ⓓ silicone oil and bornyl acetate

3. What does the word *stabilize* mean?

    Ⓐ to make more flexible   Ⓒ to make more decorative

    Ⓑ to make more solid   Ⓓ to make more playful

4. Based on what you can infer in the passage, what is the Smithsonian Institute?

    Ⓐ a scientific laboratory

    Ⓑ a museum of human accomplishments

    Ⓒ a university

    Ⓓ a museum of art

On the lines below, write your own question based on "The Birth of Silly Putty." Circle the correct picture on the left to show the level of the question you wrote.

____

____

____

____

On a separate piece of paper . . .

- Write a sentence that includes the word *substance.*

- Now that you know just some of the ways that Silly Putty is used, what would you rename it if you could? Explain your answer.

What Is Extinction?

Fossils were discovered hundreds of years ago. Fossils are the remains or impressions of things that were once living. They can be a part of an animal or plant, or they can be the whole thing. They can be footprints or other impressions. These remains or impressions are preserved in rock.

Back in the 1700s, scientists understood that these fossils were from animals and plants that lived long ago. However, many of the fossils that were found looked as if they came from species that still existed. This changed sometime in the 1800s. It was then that some of the discoveries caused scientists to scratch their heads. These newly found fossils seemed to come from animals or plants that no longer existed!

This led people to think about the idea that some species cease to exist. They become extinct. Some disappear from the planet all together. Others can become extinct in a particular area. For instance, years ago, elephant fossils were found in Italy. However, elephants didn't live in Italy. Since elephants didn't live in Italy but their remains were found there, that means that elephants must have become extinct in that area.

It has since been discovered that about 99% of all species that ever existed on Earth have become extinct. Many of these simply die out slowly over time. However, sometimes there is a "mass extinction." When this happens, half or more of the species disappear quickly. The word *quickly*, however, has a little different meaning when it refers to mass extinctions. Here, quickly means "in fewer than 2 million years."

There is a purpose to mass extinctions. These events give new species a chance to survive and thrive. Many of the species alive today got their chance after previous extinctions.

Answer the following questions about the story "What Is Extinction?" The weights show you how hard you will need to work to find each answer.

1. According to the passage, what species left a fossil in Italy that confused scientists?

Ⓐ a bobcat   Ⓒ an elephant

Ⓑ a stegosaurus   Ⓓ a wolf

2. When scientists "scratch their heads," what does that imply?

Ⓐ They are excited.   Ⓒ They are wise.

Ⓑ They are itchy.   Ⓓ They are confused.

3. Based on the passage, what does the word *impression* mean?

Ⓐ a mark made by pressing into the rock

Ⓑ a photograph

Ⓒ the bones

Ⓓ a sketch or drawing

4. Based on the passage, what would you predict happened to the dinosaurs?

Ⓐ Nothing. They are still around.

Ⓑ They became extinct in just one place.

Ⓒ They died due to a mass extinction.

Ⓓ They all sailed away.

On the lines below, write your own question based on "What Is Extinction?" Circle the correct picture on the left to show the level of the question you wrote.

____

____

____

____

____

On a separate piece of paper . . .

- Write a sentence that includes the word *purpose*.

- What might a dinosaur think if it were to appear in the world of today? Write a short essay describing a day in the life of a 21st-century dinosaur.

Gentle Giant of the Sea

The megamouth is a rare and unusual species of shark. Can you guess by its name what the most noticeable thing about the megamouth may be? That's right: its mouth! The megamouth's mouth is huge. In fact, the prefix *mega* means "big." This shark's gigantic mouth can be almost two meters (over six feet) in length.

Although megamouths are huge and look dangerous, they are actually quite peaceful. First of all, they don't attack other large animals. Instead, they are filter feeders. This means that these sharks keep their mouths open as they swim slowly along. They hope to sweep up food like jellyfish and plankton inside their enormous mouths. Their lips contain organs that light up. These organs glow and attract the food into their mouths.

However, the megamouth isn't all mouth: it has a long body, too. Its body can reach up to 18 feet long (about 5 ½ meters). That means that if you stacked four fifth graders on top of one another, they might be almost as tall as the megamouth is long! Yet despite its size and its scary-looking mouth, this shark should not be feared. Frankly, humans probably threaten it far more than it threatens us. After all, when the first megamouth was discovered in 1976, it was hanging from the anchor of a Navy ship. It had tried to swallow the anchor and was pulled up like a fish on a hook!

If you ever see a megamouth, you will have seen something very rare. Since its discovery in 1976, only about 50 of these sharks have been sighted and studied. There are scientists all over the world hoping to take a closer look at this gentle giant.

Name: ____

Answer the following questions about the story "Gentle Giant of the Sea." The weights show you how hard you will need to work to find each answer.

1. If you use the prefix *mega* in front of the root word *phone*, you get *megaphone.* Based on what you know about the prefix *mega*, what does a megaphone do?

    Ⓐ It makes your voice sound smaller.

    Ⓑ It makes your voice sound bigger.

    Ⓒ It makes your voice sound funny.

    Ⓓ It changes your phone's ringtone.

2. Why do a megamouth's lips glow?

    Ⓐ to attract food to the light   Ⓒ to tell other fish to look out!

    Ⓑ to look pretty   Ⓓ to see in the dark

3. If a building is 36 feet tall, about how many 5th graders have to stand on top of each other to equal the length of the building?

    Ⓐ 5   Ⓒ 4

    Ⓑ 3   Ⓓ 8

4. Based on the passage, what does the word *rare* mean?

    Ⓐ common   Ⓒ lonely

    Ⓑ interesting   Ⓓ uncommon

On the lines below, write your own question based on "Gentle Giant of the Sea." Circle the correct picture on the left to show the level of the question you wrote.

____

____

____

____

On a separate piece of paper . . .

- Write a sentence that includes at least two different synonyms for the word *big*.

- Based on the description of the megamouth in the passage, draw what you visualize the shark looking like as it swims along and feeds.

The History of Balloon Flight

About 130,000 spectators, including King Louis XVI, looked up into the sky above France and saw a large balloon soaring overhead. The balloon was filled with hot air. It had a basket attached to the bottom of it. The basket held the first passengers ever to fly in a hot-air balloon. The day was September 19, 1783. After eight minutes and two miles of flight, the balloon landed. All of the passengers got off safely. Who were the passengers? They were a sheep, a duck, and a rooster.

Only a year before, two men filled a silk and paper bag with hot air and watched as it rose up to the ceiling of a house. Since the hot air was less dense than the air around it, it could rise. These men, who were brothers, started experimenting with bigger and bigger bags. It was they who, under advice from the king, launched the farm animals into the sky on that September day in 1783.

The early balloon looked a little different than the hot-air balloons do of today. For one thing, it was highly decorated to impress the French royalty in the crowd.

Only two months later, the first humans flew in a hot-air balloon. It took a lot of bravery because it was still a very young science. The first man to fly in a balloon was a chemistry and physics teacher. He just went straight up and then straight back down. Why? His balloon was **tethered** to the ground with a rope. Soon, another man tried an untethered flight. He landed his balloon about five miles away from his starting point. From that point on, people began flying further and further.

Jean-Pierre Blanchard was another pioneer in the history of balloon flight. Not only that, he was also the first to use another important invention. When faced with an emergency situation, Blanchard used a parachute to successfully jump out of a balloon in mid-flight.

Answer the following questions about the story "The History of Balloon Flight." The weights show you how hard you will need to work to find each answer.

1. In what year did a duck first make a hot-air balloon flight?

    Ⓐ 1776   Ⓒ 1983

    Ⓑ 1873   Ⓓ 1783

2. What made the first balloon rise?

    Ⓐ hot air   Ⓒ ice

    Ⓑ cold air   Ⓓ silk

3. According to the passage, what quality did the first people need to have to be passengers on the early balloons?

    Ⓐ courage   Ⓒ intelligence

    Ⓑ stupidity   Ⓓ strength

4. Based on the passage, what does the word *tethered* mean?

    Ⓐ let go

    Ⓑ cut off

    Ⓒ tied to

    Ⓓ blown away

On the lines below, write your own question based on "The History of Balloon Flight." Circle the correct picture on the left to show the level of the question you wrote.

____

____

____

____

On a separate piece of paper . . .

- Write a sentence that includes the word *invention*.

- The first balloon that flew for the king had symbols on it that represented him. If you were designing a balloon, what symbols would you put on it to represent you? Draw your balloon, complete with symbols on the bag.

What Is a Geode?

A geode is a beautiful rock formation that gives you a peek inside a natural wonder. *Geo* means "earth," and a geode is a small piece of earth. Geodes are round or oval in shape. They are plain and dull on the outside but full of sparkling crystals on the inside. If you find a geode, you know that you are looking at a piece of Earth's history.

It takes a long time for a geode to form. They are formed in rounded areas like those made from the gas bubbles in volcanic rock. Over a long period of time, minerals leak into the hollow formed by the gas bubble. The mineral hardens into a crusty shell while it continues to form on the inside of what will be the geode. It can take hundreds of millions of years for a geode to actually fill in the round shape. This is why most geodes that we find today are still hollow. The crystal formations create an inside layer of beauty within the outer shell.

Many geodes have crystals on the inside that are white or even purple in color. Most are made from quartz, but some can be made from amethyst. The crystal formations form hundreds of sparkly facets. A facet is a flat surface that can reflect light and be very smooth to the touch.

Geodes can be found in many desert areas, but they have been discovered all over the world. While many American states are known for their geodes, only Iowa has named the geode its official state rock.

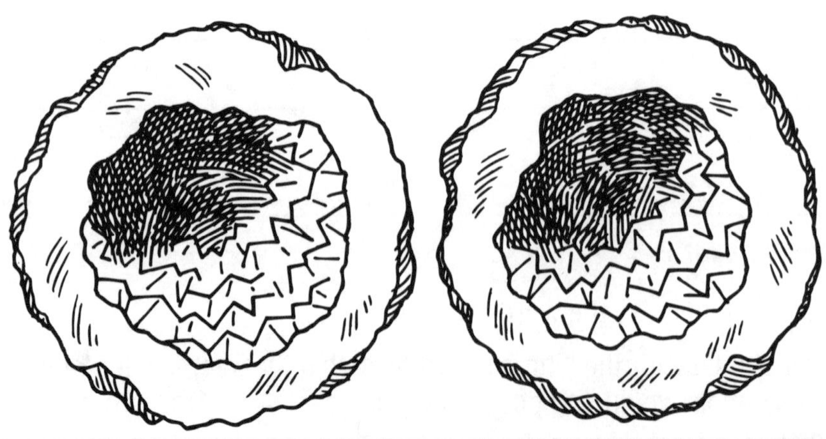

Answer the following questions about the story "What Is a Geode?" The weights show you how hard you will need to work to find each answer.

1. What does the prefix *geo* mean?

Ⓐ go   Ⓒ earth

Ⓑ maps   Ⓓ rocky

2. According to the passage, what kind of rocks have formed geodes?

Ⓐ volcanic   Ⓒ concrete

Ⓑ quartz   Ⓓ gravel

3. According to the description in the passage, what does a facet feel like?

Ⓐ spiky   Ⓒ puffy

Ⓑ sharp   Ⓓ smooth

4. According to the story, where is a location in which you would most likely might find a geode?

Ⓐ Antarctica

Ⓑ a rainforest

Ⓒ the Sahara desert

Ⓓ the Pacific Ocean

On the lines below, write your own question based on "What Is a Geode?" Circle the correct picture on the left to show the level of the question you wrote.

____

____

____

____

____

On a separate piece of paper . . .

- Write a sentence that includes the word *reflect*.

- Write a short story about finding a huge round rock in your backyard. Imagine you take a hammer and crack the rock open. Describe what you find inside.

The First Observatory

All astronomers know that the bigger the lens, the better the telescope. If the lens were big, after all, the images from space would be greater. In 1774, even William Herschel, a young musician and amateur astronomer knew that. Born in Germany, William Herschel moved to England as a young man. There, his interest in the stars really began to grow. When he tried to buy a 6-foot telescope, he discovered that no one had made an instrument that big before. So he took matters into his own hands.

In 1776, Herschel made a 10-foot long telescope through which he could see Saturn's rings. Soon after, he was the first person to see Uranus, the 5th planet we knew of in our solar system. Herschel did not stop there. He was eager to see more.

In 1786, Herschel decided to build such a big telescope that he would have to buy a house that could fit around it. He dreamed of having it be able to tilt and rotate in order to see into the heavens around him. First, he had construction crews lay a concrete foundation. Then, he had a 60-foot wooden structure built to support his telescope. It was surrounded by scaffolds like the kind you would see on a building being repaired. There were a series of pullies that could raise and lower the huge device so that one could see a particular section of sky.

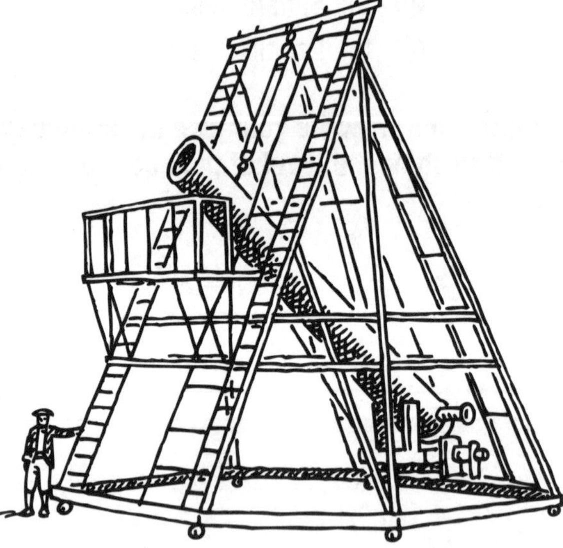

From that telescope, Herschel discovered many things. He saw a new moon around Saturn and two more of Jupiter's moons. He became one of the first people to really prove that the whole solar system moves through space.

William Herschel went from being a musician to one of the greatest astronomers who ever lived. He dreamed a big dream about building big telescopes, and he followed through with his dream to make it a reality.

Answer the following questions about the story "The First Observatory." The weights show you how hard you will need to work to find each answer.

1. What did William Herschel do before he was an astronomer?

Ⓐ He was a construction worker.   Ⓒ He was a musician.

Ⓑ He was a doctor.   Ⓓ He was a scientist.

2. How long was Herschel's first telescope?

Ⓐ 5 feet   Ⓒ 6 feet

Ⓑ 10 feet   Ⓓ 60 feet

3. Why did they add pullies to the first observatory?

Ⓐ to bring food up to the astronomers

Ⓑ to ride on like an elevator

Ⓒ to balance out the weight of the telescope

Ⓓ to raise and lower the telescope to help aim it

4. Based on the passage, what does the phrase "took matters into his own hands" mean?

Ⓐ He did it himself.

Ⓑ He hired someone to do it.

Ⓒ He gave up.

Ⓓ He threw it away.

On the lines below, write your own question based on "The First Observatory." Circle the correct picture on the left to show the level of the question you wrote.

____

____

____

____

On a separate piece of paper . . .

- Write a sentence that includes the word *rotate*.

- Where would you point a big telescope? What would you want to see up close? Describe what you would look at if you could use the world's largest telescope.

A Storytelling Tradition

North America is full of folklore. A culture's folklore includes the stories that it's people tell that teach about their traditions. The stories include the beliefs of the people, and they are usually passed down by word of mouth. That is, the older people tell the younger people. When the young people grow up, they tell their children the same stories. Every culture has its own folklore.

Native-American stories have lived through the tradition of folklore. The stories were created to help explain what happened in the world around the Native Americans. Some stories explained what happened in nature. Others explained how Earth was created. For instance, one Cherokee myth tells the story of how Earth was once a floating island. It hung on cords, and the sun was on a track that moved from east to west. This story was an explanation of a natural phenomenon.

Some stories were tales of heroes. Others were tales of "tricksters." Tricksters are characters who taught the listener how not to behave. Many of the stories included lessons. These lessons warned the people about how to behave. The lessons are called morals.

Native-American tribes passed down their folklore from father to son and mother to daughter. This way, everyone would remember the lessons from year to year. This was how the stories lived from year to year, decade to decade, and century to century.

Answer the following questions about the story "A Storytelling Tradition." The weights show you how hard you will need to work to find each answer.

1. According to the passage, folklore was passed down through "word of mouth." What can you infer is the meaning of this phrase?

Ⓐ People passed down stories using written words.
Ⓑ People passed down stories by sharing audio files.
Ⓒ People passed down stories by telling those stories to others.
Ⓓ People passed down stories by sharing books.

2. What tribe told the story of the floating island?

Ⓐ North America   Ⓒ the Cherokee
Ⓑ the Apache   Ⓓ the Mayans

3. According to the passage, what is the opposite of a hero?

Ⓐ a son   Ⓒ a daughter
Ⓑ a trickster   Ⓓ a warning

4. According to the Cherokee myth from the passage, the sun "moved on a track from east to west." What is the story trying to explain?

Ⓐ why we have the tides
Ⓑ why we have earthquakes
Ⓒ the creation of the animals
Ⓓ why the sun rises in the east and sets in the west

On the lines below, write your own question based on "A Storytelling Tradition." Circle the correct picture on the left to show the level of the question you wrote.

____

____

____

____

On a separate piece of paper . . .
- Write a sentence that includes the word *folklore.*
- What stories do you know that come from your culture?

The Guiding Rose

Can you point to the north? If not, a compass rose can help you. A compass rose isn't a new kind of flower. Instead, it is an object that helps sailors navigate. To navigate means to find a route from one place to another. Starting in the 1300s, the compass rose helped sailors navigate the seas. There are 32 points on a compass rose, and each of these points towards a different wind. The points helped travelers find the direction of the winds.

The compass rose points to the eight major winds: South, North, West, East, Southwest, Northwest, Southeast, and Northeast. There are even marks that point to winds between those major winds. These are known as the half-winds. There are also 16 quarter-winds.

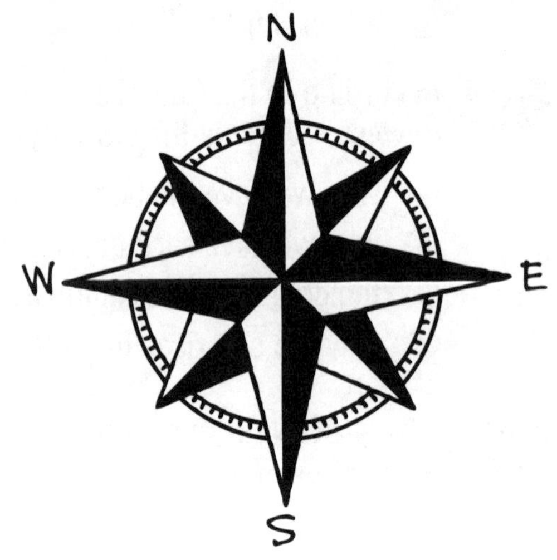

The colors you see the most on a compass rose are black and white. Why is this? It's because these colors really stand out visually. Imagine if you are on a dark ship. Even in candlelight, you would be able to see the black marks on the white background.

Nowadays, all charts and maps have some kind of compass rose. The first cartographer to draw a compass rose was Cresques Abraham of Majorca in 1375. The word *cartographer* uses the root word *graph*, which means "writing." In other words, a cartographer is a person who "writes" maps. Little did Cresques Abraham know that hundreds of years later, the compass rose he drew would still help sailors find their way across enormous seas and ultimately get to where they wanted to go.

Answer the following questions about the story "The Guiding Rose." The weights show you how hard you will need to work to find each answer.

1. To how many "major winds" does a compass rose point?

   Ⓐ 16   Ⓒ 32

   Ⓑ 4   Ⓓ 8

2. In what year did Cresques Abraham first draw a compass rose?

   Ⓐ 1901   Ⓒ 1375

   Ⓑ 1300   Ⓓ 1845

3. Based on what you know about the root word *graph*, what is an autograph?

   Ⓐ a self-portrait or drawing

   Ⓑ a car that is written on

   Ⓒ a "self writing" or signature

   Ⓓ a visual used in math

4. Based on the information from the passage, what is the meaning of *navigate*?

   Ⓐ to listen for

   Ⓑ to find one's way

   Ⓒ to watch

   Ⓓ to lose

On the lines below, write your own question based on "The Guiding Rose." Circle the correct picture on the left to show the level of the question you wrote.

____

____

____

____

____

On a separate piece of paper . . .

- Write a sentence that includes the word *navigate*.
- Why do you think this instrument is called a "rose?"

Women in the Civil War

The Civil War was the bloodiest war in American history. More Americans died in that war than in any other. In the Civil War, America fought itself. The war was between the Northern states and the Southern states, and it lasted from 1861 to 1865. Normally, when we read or hear about The Civil War, the stories are of brothers fighting against brothers. We hear about the men who fought each other. However, there were also women involved in this war.

Rose Greenhow was a spy for the South. She was a socialite. That means she went to parties, hosted functions, and made friends with people who were making key decisions during the war. Using her connections, Rose was able to learn about some of the North's military plans. She smuggled this information to the soldiers in Richmond, Virginia. Rose Greenhow was credited for helping the South win the battle at Bull Run.

Dorothea Dix became the head of the North's nursing service. She demanded that the nurses be strong and prepared for the horrors of war. She also became one of the first people to fight for mental institutions. These were hospitals specifically set up for those with mential disorders. During the war, Dorothea Dix and her team of nurses treated wounded soldiers from both the North and the South. She supported the North, but she felt that all wounded soldiers deserved to be helped.

Clara Barton was a nurse who didn't just work in a hospital. Instead, she traveled to the frontline of the battles. She helped the soldiers injured on the battlefield. After the war, Clara spent many years working to found the American Red Cross. It was dedicated to helping people caught in wars and other disasters. The American Red Cross is still an important organization today.

By the end of the Civil War, over 600,000 soldiers were dead, slavery was abolished, and the country needed to be rebuilt. In other words, slavery was made illegal, and the people needed to work to unite the country. The country needed to come together again. The women of The Civil War played a crucial role in this part of their country's history, too.

Answer the following questions about the story "Women in the Civil War." The weights show you how hard you will need to work to find each answer.

1. In what year did the Civil War end?

    Ⓐ 1985   Ⓒ 1861

    Ⓑ 1856   Ⓓ 1865

2. Rose Greenhow spied for _________________.

    Ⓐ the North   Ⓒ the South

    Ⓑ the Lakers   Ⓓ the King of England

3. Based on the passage, the word *unite* means

    Ⓐ "to bring together."

    Ⓑ "to pull apart."

    Ⓒ "to invite."

    Ⓓ "to retreat."

4. From the passage, you can infer that Clara Barton

    Ⓐ was born in 1861.

    Ⓑ was a spy for the North.

    Ⓒ did not die in the Civil War.

    Ⓓ was in the battle at Bull Run.

On the lines below, write your own question based on "Women in the Civil War." Circle the correct picture on the left to show the level of the question you wrote.

____

____

____

____

____

On a separate piece of paper . . .

- Write a sentence that includes the word *abolished.*
- What is a cause that you feel strongly about? Write about an issue you feel is worth fighting for.

Which Holiday Is This?

The people of the United States celebrate many holidays. Everyone who lives in the U.S. seems to know when holidays like Halloween and Thanksgiving will happen. But there are three holidays that people mix up all the time. The first is Veterans Day. The second is Memorial Day. The third is Labor Day. People always get confused about which one is which. The fact is that they are all three national holidays that honor different things. A national holiday means that the whole nation celebrates or honors that day. For instance, on each one, Americans get a Monday off in order to think about the purpose of that holiday. However, it can be confusing to know which one is being celebrated and when.

Veterans Day is on November 11th of each year. It honors people who have served the United States during war. The people being honored could be alive or dead. President Calvin Coolidge declared it a national holiday in 1926. On Veterans Day, one might participate in or attend a parade celebrating the military. People fly their American flags and show their patriotism.

Memorial Day is observed on the last Monday in May. It honors all the American soldiers who have died. It actually began after the Civil War. In the Civil War, the northern part of the country was fighting the southern part of the country. But once it was over, America wanted to remember all those who fought from both sides. On Memorial Day, one might place flowers on the grave of a soldier who has passed.

Labor Day is the first Monday in September. It honors all the workers in the country who have helped to build America. It became a national holiday in 1894. Typically, we celebrate this end-of-the-summer holiday by having a final party or picnic. It's the way we all start the new school year and send off the summer season until the next June.

All three holidays are important to America. All three are more than just a day Americans get to stay home from school or work.

Answer the following questions about the story "Which Holiday Is This?" The weights show you how hard you will need to work to find each answer.

1. In what month is Labor Day celebrated?

Ⓐ May

Ⓑ September

Ⓒ January

Ⓓ April

2. Which president declared Veterans Day a national holiday?

Ⓐ Reagan

Ⓑ Coolidge

Ⓒ Roosevelt

Ⓓ Clinton

3. Based on the information in the passage, the word *memorial* might mean

Ⓐ "thinking of soldiers who are alive."

Ⓑ "honoring soldiers who are currently fighting in wars."

Ⓒ "feeling grateful to all Americans."

Ⓓ "remembering soldiers who have died in battle."

4. What were the two sides that fought during the Civil War?

Ⓐ the West and East

Ⓑ the Americans and Russians

Ⓒ the French and British

Ⓓ the North and South

On the lines below, write your own question based on "Which Holiday Is This?" Circle the correct picture on the left to show the level of the question you wrote.

____

____

____

____

On a separate piece of paper . . .

- Write a sentence that includes the word *honor*.

- If you could designate a holiday, what holiday would you create? What or who would you honor?

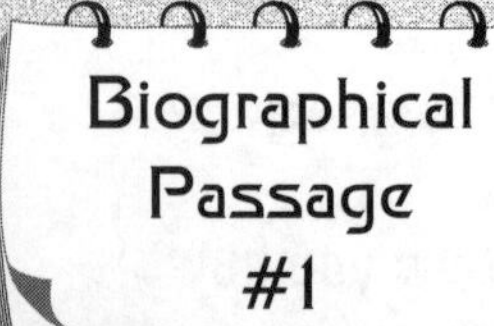

A Writer Who Lives On

William Shakespeare was born in England in 1564. He died 52 years later, but to this day, he is thought of as one of the greatest writers of all time. In all, Shakespeare penned about 38 full plays, 154 sonnets, and various other poems. Some of his most famous works have been produced over and over again as both plays and movies.

Earlier in his career, Shakespeare was both an actor and a playwright. He wrote about many different time periods, from the Renassaince to Ancient Greek times. His words transcend generations. The prefix *trans* means "across" or "beyond." So, this means that his words are read across many years because they still have meaning and importance for so many people to this day.

Shakespeare's plays are often put into one of three groups. There are the histories that center on the royalty of certain countries. There are the tragedies that center on stories full of sorrow and terrible situations. Finally, there are comedies that center on themes of mixed-up wackiness and humor. Here are some of his most famous plays:

- ***Romeo and Juliet*** – This tragedy is the story of two teenagers who fall in love. The catch is that their families are enemies, so Romeo and Juliet feel they have to keep their love a secret. The struggle between their families results in tragedy for the young lovers.

- ***A Midsummer Night's Dream*** – This play is both a comedy and a fantasy about two young couples who get lost in the woods. There, the fairies bewitch them. They wake up thinking it's all a crazy dream, but in reality, life is like a dream sometimes.

- ***Hamlet*** – This tragedy is about a young prince who dislikes the decisions his family has made to become powerful. He questions his own role in their family. Over 50 film versions of *Hamlet* have been made!

- ***Julius Caesar*** – This play is a version of the Roman ruler's life. His friends betray him, but his memory lives on in the words of Shakespeare. It's a version of history that allows the viewer or reader to understand a little more about why his friends had to be the ones to take him down.

- ***Henry V*** – This play follows the young King Henry as he proves to his followers that he can be a great leader. He spends the play making decisions so that his people will trust him, follow him, and fight for him.

Answer the following questions about the story "A Writer Who Lives On." The weights show you how hard you will need to work to find each answer.

1. In which of these years could William Shakespeare have died?

   Ⓐ 1512   Ⓒ 1616

   Ⓑ 1564   Ⓓ 1626

2. The story says that Shakespeare's plays can be categorized under three groups: tragedies, histories, and _______________.

   Ⓐ mysteries   Ⓒ comedies

   Ⓑ romances   Ⓓ fantasies

3. Which of these words from the passage is a synonym for *penned*?

   Ⓐ read   Ⓒ transcended

   Ⓑ wrote   Ⓓ centered

4. The passage mentions that one of these characters comes from a play that is a history. Which one?

   Ⓐ Romeo   Ⓒ Julius Caesar

   Ⓑ Juliet   Ⓓ Hamlet

On the lines below, write your own question based on "A Writer Who Lives On." Circle the correct picture on the left to show the level of the question you wrote.

____

____

____

____

____

On a separate piece of paper . . .

- Write a sentence that includes the word *transcend*.

- William Shakespeare once wrote, "To thine own self be true." What do you think this means?

Ben's Words of Wisdom

Benjamin Franklin is a famous American who did a lot of things. He helped shape America when it was a young country. He was an inventor. He thought up such inventions as swim fins, bifocals, the Post Office, and the lightning rod. He was also an author and philosopher. A philosopher is a person who thinks about the problems of life. Many of Benjamin's thoughts became witticisms. A witticism is a clever saying. Ben saw that people might remember lessons better if they learned them in a fun way.

Here is a list of just some of Ben's many witticisms:

- **"Lost time is never found again."**

  Franklin wrote this to teach us not to waste time.

- **"How few there are who have the courage enough to own their faults, or resolution enough to mend them."**

  Franklin believed that it took a great person to know his or her flaws (things they weren't good at doing). It also took an even greater person to then do something about those flaws.

- **"By failing to prepare, you are preparing to fail."**

  This quote means that you should plan for how to be successful at something. If you don't, then you are making it likely that you will not succeed at it. Always think ahead.

- **"Either write something worth reading or do something worth writing."**

  He is telling us here that we need to do something valuable with our lives. Make your time meaningful.

Ben's sayings made sense for people in his time. They still make sense today! He thought of the lessons that needed to be learned, and he wrote about them in a way that people could remember. Maybe you can do this, too!

Answer the following questions about the story "Ben's Words of Wisdom." The weights show you how hard you will need to work to find each answer.

1. According to the passage, what is a witticism?

     Ⓐ a boring book   Ⓒ a sad song

     Ⓑ a clever saying   Ⓓ a historic document

2. According to the passage, Benjamin Franklin wrote about lessons we should all learn. What can you infer about how Benjamin Franklin lived?

     Ⓐ He tried to not waste time.

     Ⓑ He tried to make his life meaningful.

     Ⓒ He thought ahead.

     Ⓓ All of the above are correct.

3. Based on the passage, what did Benjamin Franklin not invent?

     Ⓐ the bifocals   Ⓒ the lightning rod

     Ⓑ the garden hose   Ⓓ swim fins

4. According to the passage, what would Benjamin Franklin consider to be a flaw?

     Ⓐ running late   Ⓒ swimming

     Ⓑ reading mall   Ⓓ writing sayings

On the lines below, write your own question based on "Ben's Words of Wisdom." Circle the correct picture on the left to show the level of the question you wrote.

____

____

____

____

On a separate piece of paper . . .

- Write a sentence that includes the word *meaningful*.

- Think about a moral, a message, a theme, or a lesson that you would want other people to learn. Write a witticism of your own to help people remember the lesson.

An Early Start on Success

Michael Dell is the inventor and founder of Dell Computer. This company is the world's largest maker of PC computers. When he was young, Michael Dell had a curiosity about technology and business that few people had. At 12 years old, he worked at a restaurant washing dishes. He used the money he earned there to build his stamp collection. At 15 years old, he decided to take apart an old Apple computer. He wanted to see what made it work. By doing that, he learned a lot about computers. He learned how to build them and also how to improve them. In high school, he earned almost $20,000 helping a newspaper find new customers. He did this by going through lists of data. His interest in numbers combined with his interest in technology.

By the time Dell was in college, he was building and selling computers to students from his own dorm room. His schoolmates got a computer that didn't cost much, and they had a person to talk to for help and support. This idea was the start of a very successful company for Dell.

Soon, Dell began building and selling his computers full time. During its first full year of selling the computers, Dell's company became very prosperous. It made a lot of computers and a lot of money. By 2000, Dell was a billionaire. He even wrote a book to tell other people about his path to success.

At one point, Dell was the youngest leader of a Fortune 500 company. Fortune 500 is a yearly list of successful companies. These companies make the list because of how much money they earn.

In 2004, Michael Dell retired as the head of the company. He and his wife spent a lot of their money helping others. They donated to such places as universities and to victims of natural disasters.

As for the company, it had its ups and downs once Dell left. As a result, Dell returned in 2007 to lead the company that he helped rise to fame. It seems there is a new chapter to the Dell story that remains unwritten.

Answer the following questions about the story "An Early Start on Success." The weights show you how hard you will need to work to find each answer.

1. How old was Michael Dell when he first bought and took apart an Apple computer?

   Ⓐ 12   Ⓒ 15

   Ⓑ 37   Ⓓ 51

2. Why was Dell on the Fortune 500 list?

   Ⓐ He built a nice computer

   Ⓑ He gave to many charities

   Ⓒ He could name the parts of every computer

   Ⓓ His company earned a lot of money

3. According to the passage, what does the word *prosperous* mean?

   Ⓐ having success   Ⓒ full of magic

   Ⓑ well constructed   Ⓓ being young

4. What can you infer is the meaning of the phrase "there is a new chapter to the Dell story that remains unwritten?"

   Ⓐ Dell's story has already been written.

   Ⓑ Dell's story has never been read.

   Ⓒ Everyone knows how the story ends.

   Ⓓ Nobody knows how the story will end.

On the lines below, write your own question based on "An Early Start on Success." Circle the correct picture on the left to show the level of the question you wrote.

____

____

____

____

On a separate piece of paper . . .

- Write a sentence that includes the word *curiosity*.

- If you could build any machine, what would it do? Describe your new machine.

The Writer on Every Shelf

Look on your bookshelves at school and at home, and pay particular attention to which genres you see. A genre is a category of book. Look at your Fantasy section. Maybe you'll see *Bright Shadow* or *Perloo the Bold*. Look at your Historical Fiction section. Maybe you'll see *Crispin: Cross of Lead* or *The True Confessions of Charlotte Doyle* or *The Fighting Ground*. Look at your Young Adult section, Mystery section, and your picture books. Maybe you'll see *Nothing But the Truth*, *The Man Who Was Poe,* or *Silent Movie*. Chances are, you have at least one of these books in your collection. So, other than that, what do all of these books have in common? They were all written by a man named Avi.

Avi is not his real name, but he won't reveal what his real name is. That is because when he was about a year old, his twin sister called him "Avi," and it stuck for good. "Avi" has become his pseudonym. The prefix *pseudo* means "false" or "fake." The suffix *nym* means "name." In other words, "Avi" is this writer's fake name.

Avi was born in 1937 in Brooklyn, New York. As a young boy, he was shy. He didn't like sports much, but he used his imagination by getting lost in books of all kinds. He read picture books, chapter books, comics, and listened to tons of kids' radio programs. This history of loving to read helped fuel his imagination as a writer.

Avi has won many major literary awards, including the following:

- **The Newbery Award** – This is awarded to the author who has given the most to children's literature during that given year.

- **The Boston-Globe Horn Book Award** – This is for being a prolific author in children's and young adult literature

- **The Scott O'Dell Historical Fiction Award** – This one is given to the children's author who builds up children's interest in events that make up the history of the United States.

Avi is a prolific writer. That means that he has written a large number of books. And he isn't done yet. He continues to write new books for new readers to discover. What books by Avi have you read?

Answer the following questions about the story "The Writer on Every Shelf." The weights show you how hard you will need to work to find each answer.

1. In what year was Avi born?

   Ⓐ 1397
   Ⓒ 2007
   Ⓑ 1937
   Ⓓ 1973

2. According to the passage, Avi is prolific. Based on this, what would he most likely do in the future?

   Ⓐ give himself a new name
   Ⓑ write one or two more books
   Ⓒ become a musician
   Ⓓ write a lot more books

3. In the phrase "helped fuel his imagination," what is a synonym for the word *fuel*?

   Ⓐ destroy
   Ⓒ contain
   Ⓑ imagine
   Ⓓ feed

4. Which of Avi's books below does the story say is historical fiction?

   Ⓐ *Perloo the Bold*
   Ⓑ *Silent Movie*
   Ⓒ *The Fighting Ground*
   Ⓓ *The Man Who Was Poe*

On the lines below, write your own question based on "The Writer on Every Shelf." Circle the correct picture on the left to show the level of the question you wrote.

____

____

____

____

On a separate piece of paper . . .

- Write a sentence that includes the word *pseudonym*.

- If you could write any kind of genre of book, what would it be and why?

Racing Into History

Danica Patrick is one of the most successful racecar drivers in the world. However, what makes her really special is that she is one of only a few women who race cars professionally. Danica was born on March 25, 1982, in Wisconsin. She first began racing go-carts with her sister at the age of 10. When she grew up, she began to pursue more serious car races.

The Indianapolis 500 is one of racing's most prestigious events. This means that it is a well respected event. In 2005, Danica took part in this prestigious race. She was only the fourth woman to ever do that. She came in fourth place. No woman had ever done so well in this race.

In 2013, she won the timed trials at the Daytona 500. A timed trial is when a racer speeds his or her car around the track and tries to beat the best time. The winner could then receive the pole position for the main race. The pole position is really important because it allows your car to start a race in the best spot on the track. Danica became the first woman to ever win the pole position for the Daytona 500. She later raced across the finish line to win eighth place in the highly competitive race.

Her fame has won her many awards. It has also won her other opportunities. She has appeared in many commercials, music videos, and television shows. She's even published a book about her life.

Despite her racing success Danica won't be satisfied until she comes out on top. "I was brought up to be the fastest driver, not the fastest girl," she said.

Answer the following questions about the story "Racing Into History." The weights show you how hard you will need to work to find each answer.

1. In what year did Danica Patrick first race the Indianapolis 500?

    Ⓐ 1982   Ⓒ 2005

    Ⓑ 1905   Ⓓ 2013

2. What does it mean that it was a "highly competitive race"?

    Ⓐ it was raised off the ground

    Ⓑ everyone was trying hard to win

    Ⓒ it was really expensive to race

    Ⓓ it was a complicated event

3. What does the word *prestigious* mean?

    Ⓐ well respected   Ⓒ fast

    Ⓑ frowned upon   Ⓓ famous

4. How can you infer Danica felt after winning the pole position for the Daytona 500?

    Ⓐ frightened

    Ⓑ unhappy

    Ⓒ brave

    Ⓓ proud

On the lines below, write your own question based on "Racing Into History." Circle the correct picture on the left to show the level of the question you wrote.

____

____

____

____

On a separate piece of paper . . .

- Write a sentence that includes the word *achieved*.

- If you were a famous athlete, what other opportunities would you pursue? Would you be in commercials or television shows? Name some things you think you might do.

A Better Way to Search

How do you search for information on the Internet? Do you go to the URL for the main Google homepage? This can be found at *www.google.com*. Once there, do you type in a topic? Does a massive list of the websites pop up? Let's say, for example, you are doing a report on how the American Revolution was won. You type "American Revolution" into the main search bar. Within .15 seconds, you get approximately 348,000,000 results! You certainly aren't going to look through all those sites. Most of them won't even really apply to your topic. It can take a lot of work to sift through all of this unhelpful information.

Fortunately, Google has an option. It allows you to make your computer do much more work for you. It's called Google Advanced Search. You can find it at *http://www.google.com/advanced_search*.

This tool allows you to make your search much more specific. By doing that, you'll find that the results are far more helpful to your research. They will be more reliable. Here are just some fields that you can fill in to make the results more trustworthy:

1. You can ask a question.
2. You can use more specific keywords.
3. You can narrow the dates of when the information was published.
4. You can search by file type (.doc, Powerpoint, .pdf, etc.).
5. You can search for websites in a particular language.
6. You can search for books only.
7. You can search for papers written only by graduate students or professors.
8. You can search by reading level (Basic, Intermediate, Advanced).

Using this tool might just whittle your 350 million hits down to a handful. Wouldn't that make your searching go a lot more smoothly?

Answer the following questions about the story "A Better Way to Search." The weights show you how hard you will need to work to find each answer.

1. Based on the passage, what does the word *reliable* mean?

   Ⓐ advanced   Ⓒ massive

   Ⓑ trustworthy   Ⓓ related

2. Which of these categories is not mentioned as one you can adjust to make your search more dependable?

   Ⓐ keywords   Ⓒ text colors

   Ⓑ publishing dates   Ⓓ reading levels

3. Based on what you learned about Google Advanced Search, what is the most specific search phrase that the student can use for his or her research?

   Ⓐ "The American Revolution"   Ⓒ "The History of America"

   Ⓑ "Revolutions"   Ⓓ "How did we win the American Revolution?"

4. At what URL would you find Google Advanced Search?

   Ⓐ *www.google.com*

   Ⓑ *http://en.wikipedia.org/wiki/AmericanRevolution*

   Ⓒ *images.google.com/*

   Ⓓ *http://www.google.com/advanced_search*

On the lines below, write your own question based on "A Better Way to Search." Circle the correct picture on the left to show the level of the question you wrote.

____

____

____

____

____

On a separate piece of paper . . .

- Write a sentence that includes the word *specific*.

- Imagine you are researching a Native-American civilization. What might be a specific keyword search term that you can use if you are focusing your research on their rites and traditions?

Reading an Infographic

An infographic is a way to display data. It uses symbols and pictures to present facts. The purpose of it can just be to inform. An infographic can also be used to persuade a reader. It can be very effective at doing this.

Just look at the word *infographic*. It gives you the two main elements that define it: *info* and *graphic*. In other words, an infographic is made up of information and pictures.

You can find infographics everywhere these days. They are used in every newspaper and on many websites. They are often used to display factual evidence. This comes in many forms: data, graphs, quotes, statistics, or even photographs. You will also find infographics online because they help readers understand big ideas.

So let's say you are writing an essay on the dangers of texting and driving. You begin your essay with this sentence: *Texting and driving is a dangerous trend that threatens many lives every year.* In the body of your essay, you include this infographic:

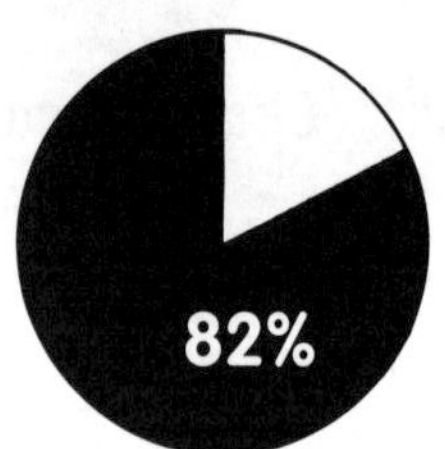

The percentage of American teenagers who own a cell phone.

The percentage of teenage drivers who admit to texting while driving.

The minimum amount of time you aren't paying attention to the road while texting and driving.

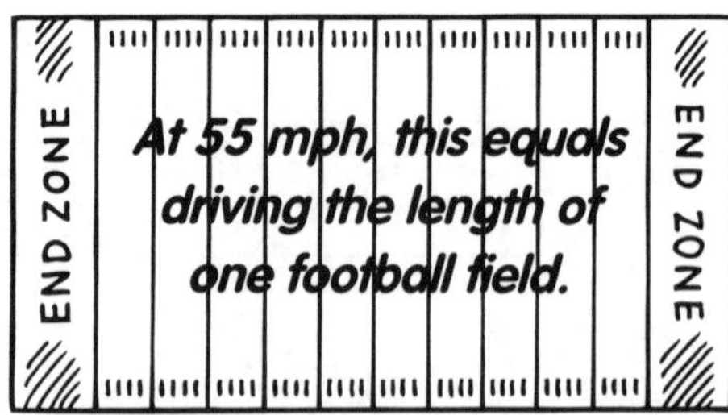

You then end your essay by asking young people to sign a contract promising not to text and drive. Your words are still important, but the infographic really improves your argument. You have used today's language of images and graphics to present evidence. In a glance, your reader can understand the reasons behind your stance.

Answer the following questions about the story "Reading an Infographic." The weights show you how hard you will need to work to find each answer.

1. What is not an example of factual evidence?

   Ⓐ data   Ⓒ opinions

   Ⓑ pie charts   Ⓓ statistics

2. Looking at the infographic, what percent of teens have admitted to texting while driving?

   Ⓐ 82   Ⓒ 34

   Ⓑ 43   Ⓓ 55

3. Based on the infographic, what is used to represent the distance one drives in five seconds?

   Ⓐ two car lengths   Ⓒ five car lengths

   Ⓑ a football field   Ⓓ a cell phone

4. After reading the passage, which of these best describes the purpose of an infographic?

   Ⓐ to entertain and persuade

   Ⓑ to inform and excite

   Ⓒ to persuade and argue

   Ⓓ to inform and persuade

On the lines below, write your own question based on "Reading an Infographic." Circle the correct picture on the left to show the level of the question you wrote.

____

____

____

____

On a separate piece of paper . . .

- Write a sentence that includes the word *display*.

- When you need information about a topic, would you rather just read words, or would you rather have the information presented to you as an infographic? Give reasons for your answer.

A Way to Show Time

A timeline is a picture that represents time. It can quickly show you the major events that have happened over a 100-year period in a country's history. It could represent a much smaller or much larger period of time, too. Timelines are versatile in this way. They can be used in many ways to give a lot of information with a minimum amount of words.

There are different kinds of timelines. Some are rays. Rays begin with a starting mark, like a period. The period represents a moment in time. A ray ends with the symbol of an arrow. That means that time continues beyond the length of the line. If the timeline is in the form of a straight line with two arrows at the end, then that means that it is showing you a section of time.

In the example below, each mark shows a decade. The timeline shows some important events that took place during each 10-year period of the 19th century in America.

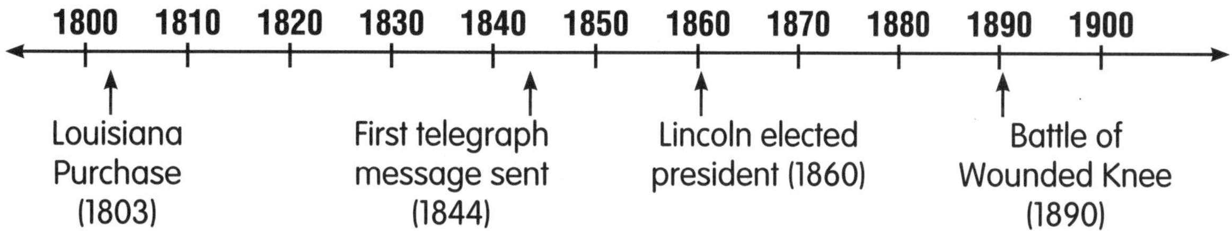

A timeline doesn't always have to be horizontal. It can also be vertical. The timeline below was created by a 5th-grader to show some of the events that took place on a recent Saturday.

Time	Event
8:00	Woke up and ate breakfast
9:30	Played in a soccer game at Wilson Park
11:45	Ate lunch with the team after the game
1:30	Played video games at home
3:00	Worked on school project
4:30	Talked on the phone with a friend
6:00	Ate dinner with family
9:45	Time for bed!

Answer the following questions about the story "A Way to Show Time." The weights show you how hard you will need to work to find each answer.

1. Based on the passage, what does the word *horizontal* mean?

   Ⓐ up and down   Ⓒ around

   Ⓑ through   Ⓓ across

2. What kind of timeline could begin with a starting mark?

   Ⓐ a rod   Ⓒ a line

   Ⓑ a ray   Ⓓ a pole

3. Based on the passage, which of the following time periods is a decade?

   Ⓐ 1900–2000   Ⓒ 1990–1999

   Ⓑ 2010–2100   Ⓓ 1800–1803

4. Looking at the 5th-grader's timeline, which event took place before lunch?

   Ⓐ played video games

   Ⓑ played a soccer game

   Ⓒ talked on phone with friend

   Ⓓ worked on school project

On the lines below, write your own question based on "A Way to Show Time." Circle the correct picture on the left to show the level of the question you wrote.

____

____

____

____

On a separate piece of paper . . .

- Write a sentence that includes the word *vertical*.

- What would a timeline of your day look like? Create one for a recent Saturday or Sunday.

A Show of Shadows

First, turn out the lights, then hold your hand up in front of a flashlight. Do you see your shadow on the wall? Now try to position your hands so that the shadow they create looks like a crab claw or a flapping bird. Basically, this is how shadow puppets are created. A shadow puppet uses light and darkness to make pictures for an audience. A sheet blocks the puppets. The audience cannot see the objects that are casting the shadows, and this makes a show of shadow puppets different than most puppet shows. In this kind of show, the shadow is the only thing the audience sees.

The first known shadow puppet show was performed during the Han Dynasty in China. It was created in order to entertain the emperor. From these beginnings, this kind of theater grew as an art form, and now over 20 countries have shadow puppet theaters. It is a form of artistic expression that is very much alive.

You don't have to be a professional to create a shadow puppet show. You just need the following supplies: a thin screen, a bright light, and at least one puppet. The puppet can be paper cut out in a shape and taped on a stick. The stick allows the puppeteer to move it around the scene. The sheet hangs in front of the audience. It blocks the puppeteer from their view. The light is behind the screen. The puppet casts a shadow on the screen. For the audience, it appears that the shadow is moving around like a real performer.

It can be really fun to make a shadow puppet show. It's also great to just be in the audience and watch one.

Answer the following questions about the story "A Show of Shadows." The weights show you how hard you will need to work to find each answer.

1. What are the materials needed to create a shadow puppet show?

Ⓐ paper, stick, screen, tape, light   Ⓒ paper, stick, screen, glue

Ⓑ paper, stick, stage, tape, light   Ⓓ costumes, stick, stage

2. Based on the passage, where does the screen go?

Ⓐ In between the puppet and the puppeteer

Ⓑ In between the audience and the puppet

Ⓒ In between the light and the puppet

Ⓓ In between the puppeteer and the light

3. Where did shadow puppets first come from?

Ⓐ Japan   Ⓒ England

Ⓑ France   Ⓓ China

4. Why do you need the light behind the puppet?

Ⓐ to cast a shadow on the screen

Ⓑ to make sure the puppeteer can see

Ⓒ to make sure the audience can see the puppeteer

Ⓓ to create a heat source for the theater

On the lines below, write your own question based on "A Show of Shadows." Circle the correct picture on the left to show the level of the question you wrote.

____

____

____

____

____

___

On a separate piece of paper . . .

- Write a sentence that includes the word *shadow*.

- Shadow puppets are described as being "a form of artistic expression." What form of "artistic expression" do you like best, and why? (Some other forms could be music, film, painting, drawing, etc.)

Answer Key

Accept appropriate responses for the final three entries on the question-and-answer pages.

The Birth of Silly Putty (page 11)
1. D
2. C
3. B
4. B

What Is Extinction? (page 13)
1. C
2. D
3. A
4. C

Gentle Giant of the Sea (page 15)
1. B
2. A
3. D
4. D

The History of Balloon Flight (page 17)
1. D
2. A
3. A
4. C

What Is a Geode? (page 19)
1. C
2. A
3. D
4. C

The First Observatory (page 21)
1. C
2. B
3. D
4. A

A Storytelling Tradition (page 23)
1. C
2. C
3. B
4. D

The Guiding Rose (page 25)
1. D
2. C
3. C
4. B

Women in the Civil War (page 27)
1. D
2. C
3. A
4. C

Which Holiday Is This? (page 29)
1. B
2. B
3. D
4. D

A Writer Who Lives On (page 31)
1. C
2. C
3. B
4. C

Ben's Words of Wisdom (page 33)
1. B
2. D
3. B
4. A

An Early Start on Success (page 35)
1. C
2. D
3. A
4. D

The Writer on Every Shelf (page 37)
1. B
2. D
3. D
4. C

Racing Into History (page 39)
1. C
2. B
3. A
4. D

A Better Way to Search (page 41)
1. B
2. C
3. D
4. D

Reading an Infographic (page 43)
1. C
2. C
3. B
4. D

A Way to Show Time (page 45)
1. D
2. B
3. C
4. B

A Show of Shadows (page 47)
1. A
2. B
3. D
4. A